GW00494519

ABOUT THE AUTHOR

Erica Gillingham is a queer poet & writer living in London, England, via Siskiyou County, California. She is a bookseller at Gay's The Word bookshop, Books Editor for *DIVA*, and Poetry Editor for *The Signal House Edition*. Her poems have been published by Cipher Press and Pilot Press as well as *Impossible Archetype, Untitled: Writing* and other journals, and she has essays in *Queer Love, Queer Life* (Muswell Press, November 2021) and *So Hormonal* (Monstrous Regiment, August 2020). Erica also has a PhD in lesbian love stories in young adult literature.

The Human Body is a Hive is her debut pamphlet.

www.ericagillingham.com

The Human Body is a Hive

Erica Gillingham

VERVE
POETRY PRESS
BIRMINGHAM

PUBLISHED BY VERVE POETRY PRESS
https://vervepoetrypress.com
mail@vervepoetrypress.com

FIRST PUBLISHED MAR 2022

Printed and bound in the UK

ISBN: 978-1-913917-07-4

CONTENTS

Acknowledgements

The Human Body is a Hive

for Alex, my love
who walks alongside me in laughter and sorrow

I: Pheromones

Orange Peels, Tectonic Shifts

Against the café table top,
you spread out your fingertips, press
your palms to its surface and ask me
to imagine an array of orange peel pieces
standing in for tectonic plates;
a classroom explanation of mapping projections
turned discussion of the earth's crust.

I listen, attentive yet strained,
an unexpected flush rising in my belly;
conjure the sweet smell of orange oil
on your fingers, the soft edges of pith,
ache for my pale skin to be the mantle
underneath the fault lines of your hands.

The Gallery Floor

On days when we'd go to the galleries,
I chose my shoes based on their sound
against the concrete or hardwood floors.
Elegant but hushed, I wanted the day's rhythm
punctuated by our companionate shuffle,
overlaid by the chatter of the patrons
and our cheeky side remarks. Spoken
in low tones during the intersection
of our orbits, we'd reveal which pictures
we would hang in our homes,
ones that left us besotted, and those
we just couldn't care less about—
a statement typically followed by a nod
and an exit into the next exhibition room.
We'd spend time together elsewhere too
but, in the galleries, our edges became soft—
a lifting only possible with proximity,
like birds finding the upwash,
my feet barely brushing the floor.

Gladly, A Fool

Mesmerised by you in the golden hour,
the windows ajar, the warmth of the breeze,
light catching on your soft lips, a murmur,
your hand selecting the next track with ease.

Caught out, my chest releases its pressure—
our lush days of desire receding now,
needling against an aching fissure—
before the gentlest rise of strings, bows,

the pulsating resonance of the reeds—
'I am a fool for that shake in your thighs'—
flashes of bodies fulfilling their needs—
'I am a fool for that sound in your sighs'.

The chorus, the culmination, is too much—
the catch of my breath, the lack of your touch.

This Poem Wants to be a Lesbian Country Song So Bad

This poem wants to croon
from the tape deck in your pick-up truck
down that red dirt road
as you make your way to the honky-tonk
on a Saturday night,
your girl straddling the stick-shift.

It wants to be kicked and stomped
into the hardwood floor of the bar
drip with your sweat, your tequila, your beer,
and find you in the bathroom stall:
hands against the wall
belt-buckle clanging against concrete
your girl do-se-do-ing you between rounds
cause you're here for the party.

This poem wants to sneak
onto the jukebox like the river run dry
as you and she slip out the back door
drive up to the mountain clearing
and play loud and long
while you make fireworks explode
under the stripes of the white moonlight
and the blanket made of stars.

An Expedition for Love

I started by hiking into the miles of evergreen forest
followed the nearest river until it dwindled to a stream
then set off in search of the next ridge to cross—
all the while looking for her. I thought maybe she'd be
perched with a picnic for two on a rocky outcrop
a place I could scramble to meet her, slightly out of breath.

In the next valley over, I found a car with the keys
in the ignition, hopped in—and took off for the highways.
I scanned the aisles of all-night gas stations, hoped to brush
the back of her hand as we reached for a midnight snack,
sat in diners with red vinyl booths that only served pie
just in case she was there propped up against the jukebox.

I made it all the way to the coast, drawn by the waves,
the bustle of the boardwalk with sodas and funnel cakes,
the screams rising from the rickety roller coaster.
It turns out, love's hard to pick out in a crowd—
I'd only caught the bronze sheen of her hair when
she turned around, her eyes like fizzy cola, just as surprised.

Naming Our Unborn Daughters

Here's a crazy thought, I said:
what if we named our daughter
Bernadette. I've liked the name
ever since I had that counsellor
at middle school summer camp.

You, snuggled in beside me,
replied, what about Charlotte—
Charlie for short as it's done here,
starting a campaign for a spot
as a top contender on the list.

But what about Ella
or Emma, Eva or Evelyn
all style & simplicity, we said.
What about Hero or Harriet
Coraline or Lyra, literary favourites.

What about Louise, Loulou for short,
or Lucille after my great-grandmother.
What about Claire as a middle name
after your sister; Grace or Marie for us.

We pondered over our fluctuating tally,
parsed minutes on an underground train,
debated over early evening glasses of wine
with no intention of conceiving—just yet—
but knowing that when the time came
we would be ready

unless we had sons.

Minor English Goddesses

There was Mildred, goddess
of the moors, mizzle, and mist,
the blooming gorse bush and
the thistle, mistress of the manor,
long lost daughter of Daphne

sister of Margot, who was goddess
of the hedgerow, protector
of brambles and field mice,
nettles, pebbles, and footpaths,
who was once the lover of

Beatrice, goddess of the streams,
allotments, and rodents—rabbits,
badgers, rats, and moles—who
carried a scythe and gave birth
under the deep blue moon

to Rowen, goddess of the bracken,
heathers, lichens, and mosses,
guardian of the ridge tops, striding out
from dusk to dawn, wind whipping
fervently to the coastline where

Lerryn kept watch over the waves,
goddess of rock pools and tide pools,
seaweeds, fossils, and limestone,
who once threatened a gale to ruin
the most experienced of sailors.

The Muslin Moth

(Diaphora mendica, female)

The moth emerged in the soft light
of the morning, almost camouflaged
against the pearly bathroom wall.

Full of sleep and wonder, startled by its fresh presence,
I nodded in acknowledgment, a kinship with its perching.
Next morning, three red drops: a vertical line,

like dried blood. Unaware of life cycles,
I worried about potential causes of illness
while my love began to panic; I'd forgotten her fear of moths.

Quickly, then, I balanced on a corner of the bathtub
with my tools—a pint glass and a postcard—
to save them both.

The Year I Was Meant to be Pregnant

The daydreaming started in July
a child with your hair & my eyes
born at the start of a new decade
in the year of our tin anniversary.

By autumn we had our first try
began imagining the holidays
with announcements & a subtle bump
the swelling of my belly
as we lay in bed each night,
a measurable growth of our family,
the expectant cries of a summer baby.

Winter came & the light turned to
lengthening days, a second cycle, a
new hope
that the saints & turn of seasons would
prove good omens: a nestling infant
to be born at Christmas time,
the excitement much more cautious,
tentative whispers of what *could* still
happen.

Then life came to a halt, projections
of gestations slipped into another year
& only lining grew

When We Fuck With Our Fingers

When we fuck with our fingers / we are driving a manual transmission
headed west on a far-flung deserted highway / with the windows
rolled down to let in the heat, the breeze / your hand upon my thigh
and nowhere we have to be / but right here: the radio humming,
the thrum of our bodies / hurtling toward the horizon line and an
      endless sky.

When we fuck with our fingers / we are exploring *terra incognita*,
traversing the hills, the valleys, the ravines / reading the contours
for a route through the wilderness / with only each other for company
and an unquenchable thirst / until, maybe, just maybe, we crest the peak
of the continental divide / and find our way home again.

When we fuck with our fingers / we are scanning lines of poetry
finding the rhythms of iambs with our fingertips / the delight
in the breaks of this phenomenal woman / with her slant rhymes
and hive of honeybees / the rapture of repetition, repetition, repetition
offering a release of so many words / we can no longer hold onto.

When we fuck with our fingers / we are conducting an orchestra
in the finest concert halls of Europe / arranging the strings, the bass,
the breath, the timpani, from lento to crescendo / we know the melody,
we have rehearsed for days, months, years / each iteration begs
a fresh ear, the plush seats / the acoustics of the new day.

When we fuck with our fingers / we are diving from the deck
into the dark, brackish, fathomless sea / the exhilarating chill
tingling across exposed skin / the catch of the lungs and
the all-consuming freedom / of limbs and bellies and breasts
the lingering salt in the palm of my hand / long after the waves
    have subsided.

II: Honeycomb

The Human Body is a Hive

For centuries, beekeepers and philosophers were
preoccupied by questions of the queen bee's reproduction.
Hypotheses put forth of pheromones, external fertilisation,
the asexual act of parthenogenesis—until an unlikely pair
of naturalists, dependent on each other, observed the queen

       exiting the hive and arcing in concentric circles
       until she was almost microscopic to the human eye,
       until she reached the fleet of expectant drones,
       those able and present to pass on their genetic material.

She may make several trips, encounter many bees,
but this will be the only time the queen sees the sky,
feels the sun shining on her belly, when she is not
swaddled in the warmth and aroma of her workers.

       My hand on my abdomen, I imagine other scientists
       working indoors with filtered light, meticulous notes,
       unpicking the process of an egg leaving the body,
       becoming an embryo, and returning to a familiar,
       dark place with a singular, humming purpose.

In Vivo

Ready with my feet in metal stirrups, I am waiting
with a doctor, a nurse, an embryologist, and
one specially-designed plastic dish; *in vitro*.

Momentarily held under a microscope, magnified
in grey-scale on a monitor: an embryo appears—
and it is moving. A kinetic kind of cellular activity
I can barely comprehend; instead, recollections
of homemade models of cells from biology class;
vivus: alive, living, having properties of life.

My date of birth is verified, the transfer completed.
Then, a different screen shows the embryo
as a tiny, bright speck, nestled among layers
of expectant tissue; *in vivo*.

Soon, I will wonder what the difference is
between being *alive*   and *in the body*.

Greasy Spoon Conception

There is a photograph:

    a pale café counter top,
    two white plates brimming
    with an English breakfast—
    a side of hash browns,
    black pudding, extra bacon—
    two mugs of tea, milky
    with one sugar each,
    a small plate of buttered toast,
    one slice with a bite taken out.

    There are two pairs of thighs
    work trousers & blue jeans,
    rumples of a patterned
    shirt & a favourite jumper,
    nervous hands that are not
    quite sure where to rest
    because somewhere in between
    exists the potential for three

        suspended in the air

            like the pregnant silence

                after an order is called

      like the moment before

            a camera shutter clicks

Early Grief

On an unspecified date

in a two-week period

an embryo

that was   alive

died in utero

passed through the cervix
at an unknown time
in a state
that was undetectable

only incidental evidence:

hormonal changes
tenderness
a wild inability to conjure hope

before what followed—

What Waiting Feels Like

A

palimpsest

of

desire

&

regret.

Charged Particles

I carried you with me

in the taxi to Soho
to the national gallery
over a meal fit for pearly queens

at work behind the desk
on the seat in the train carriage
when curled up on the sofa

while drinking cups of tea
up the hill to the station
at rest in the garden all our own.

until the ground seemed to alter
until the flood of tears would not stop
until the hormones suddenly up & left

like the pull of a magnetic field, repolarising.

Dear Recipient

As a donor, I sometimes imagine you
on my commutes to the clinic, on leafy pavements,
in waiting rooms; gently linger on faces
as we may both do, involuntarily, one day

at the school gate, the public swimming pool,
dance classes, football matches, and birthdays—
looking for familiar signs in your child or mine:
an interest in the oceans, a talent for writing.

Like us, recipients, too, for this process to work
you require the donation of a collection of cells
by an imperfect stranger whose signature means
the radical possibility of a new life can begin.

I wonder, how many months have you waited
for the phone to ring? How often have you startled
out of daydream? How long have you carried
your body, walking bleary and broken-hearted?

Dear recipient, I give you half of what's mine
with every intention of fulfilling your wish
for a child, who I hope is every bit as curious
about the long, loving story wound within you.

Dreaming of a Frozen Embryo

Perhaps you will be well-suited for the desert:
deprived of water or ice, you will know how to
wait for the source, embed into the landscape,
maintain a clear direction toward the horizon.

Perhaps transatlantic distances will not scare you,
an ultra athlete from conception with the endurance
to achieve excellence in out-of-body experiences,
a clever combination of genetics and circumstance.

Perhaps, instead, you will seek out the frozen reaches
of the blue planet, a chilly isolation achingly familiar,
slip beneath the surface of the waves to witness the
heft of an iceberg, your tender heartbeat slowed.

Made of star stuff, like the rest of us, perhaps you, too,
will be inundated by intervals of inescapable nostalgia.

A Pregnant Vessel

A ship ferrying passengers from one
island to the next. Fishing boats,
returning. The *Argo* with its many
boards, and the vase telling its story.

Daylight on the summer equinox. A
saltwater swimming pool. Sugar cones
waiting for ice cream. A cement mixer
in a child's hand.

The pouch of a male seahorse. Throat
of a humpback whale as it lunges
towards the krill. An aquarium of
jellyfish, translucent bells pumping.

A motorcycle sidecar with a helmet.
The chambers of the heart supplying
highways of blood. The gas tank
almost on empty.

Milk bottles that held single tulips at
our wedding. A small dish with four
wells, a thin layer of phenol red. The
human body one day

                    and then not.

Let's Make a Baby With Science

We can't fuck our way to a family
so let's do the furthest thing possible
from the intimacy of our bedroom.

Let's invite a dozen medical professionals
to ask us invasive questions with varying
degrees of empathy & bedside manner.

Let's test my veins, my blood, my uterus,
my textbook ovaries until we lose track
of our week-on-week appointments.

Let's find ourselves speechless after each shot,
not knowing how to respond to each other,
syringes empty, sharp's box lying at our feet.

Let's turn down invitations to all-night discos,
weekend benders & sweaty basement raves
because we've got at-home stimulants to do.

Let's call the process a cycle, as if it's natural,
then spend two weeks worrying about having
enough piss in my bladder for the pregnancy test.

And when it doesn't work, think it should work,
we won't know why, may never know why,
then we'll do it all over again. And again.

And again.

And again.

And again.

ACKNOWLEDGEMENTS

I am grateful that these poems were first published by the following publications and queer presses: 'This Poem Wants to be a Lesbian Country Song So Bad' in *Screams & Silences*, 'Orange Peels, Tectonic Shifts' as 'Orange Peel' in *clavmag*, 'The Human Body is a Hive' in *Impossible Archetype: Issue #7*, 'Let's Make a Baby with Science' and 'Dear Recipient' as 'The Receiver' in *Untitled: Voices 1:1*, 'The Gallery Floor' and 'When We Fuck with Our Fingers' in *There Will Always Be Nights Like This (Cipher Shorts #1)*, 'A Pregnant Vessel' in *a queer anthology of healing*, 'Minor English Goddesses' and 'The Muslin Moth' in *The Signal House Edition: Issue 7*, and 'Greasy Spoon Conception' in *Fourteen Poems: Issue 6*. Thank you to those supportive editors and early readers. There have been so many opportunities had and connections made because of your dedication to raising up new voices.

It is wondrous to me that these poems now inhabit a tangible thing and I am indebted to many fine folks who have helped usher them into the wider world. Thank you to Stuart Bartholomew for being annoyed when I didn't send you my work. Thank you to Jo Flynn for taking such care with the first draft and my fledgling step back into the world of poetry. (Thank you, Danielle Mustarde, for being there, too.) Thank you to Julia Hiser, Keith Jarrett, Mary Jean Chan, Jo Morris Dixon and Fen Coles for reading early drafts and being so encouraging. Thank you, especially, to Farnaz Fatemi for bringing your editorial precision and fierce love to its final iterations; what a joy to see our work making their way into print together after so long.

Thank you, too, to those who have been alongside my wife Alex and me during our months and months of fertility treatments: our London community, especially, Fen & Kerry, Julie, Clare, Jo, Deborah & Aren, Jim, Uli, Em, Simon & Drew, Jenn & Ellis, Alison, Mary Jean & Jo, and many others who shared a meal or offered a hug during that time; our friends on the West Coast, particularly, Lucy & Ruth, Katie, Kate, Julia and DanRae; and our wonderfully supportive and loving families on both sides of the pond.

Finally, thank you to Alex, who has taught me more about love than I ever thought possible. From those early road trips to the birth of our baby boy, everything is better (and imaginable) with you right by my side.

ABOUT VERVE POETRY PRESS

Verve Poetry Press is a quite new and already award-winning press that focussed initially on meeting a local need in Birmingham - a need for the vibrant poetry scene here in Brum to find a way to present itself to the poetry world via publication. Co-founded by Stuart Bartholomew and Amerah Saleh, it now publishes poets from all corners of the UK and beyond - poets that speak to the city's varied and energetic qualities and will contribute to its many poetic stories.

Added to this is a colourful pamphlet series, many featuring poets who have performed at our sister festival - and a poetry show series which captures the magic of longer poetry performance pieces by festival alumni such as Polarbear, Matt Abbott and Genevieve Carver.

The press has been voted Most Innovative Publisher at the Saboteur Awards, and has won the Publisher's Award for Poetry Pamphlets at the Michael Marks Awards.

Like the festival, we strive to think about poetry in inclusive ways and embrace the multiplicity of approaches towards this glorious art.

https://vervepoetrypress.com
@VervePoetryPres
mail@vervepoetrypress.com